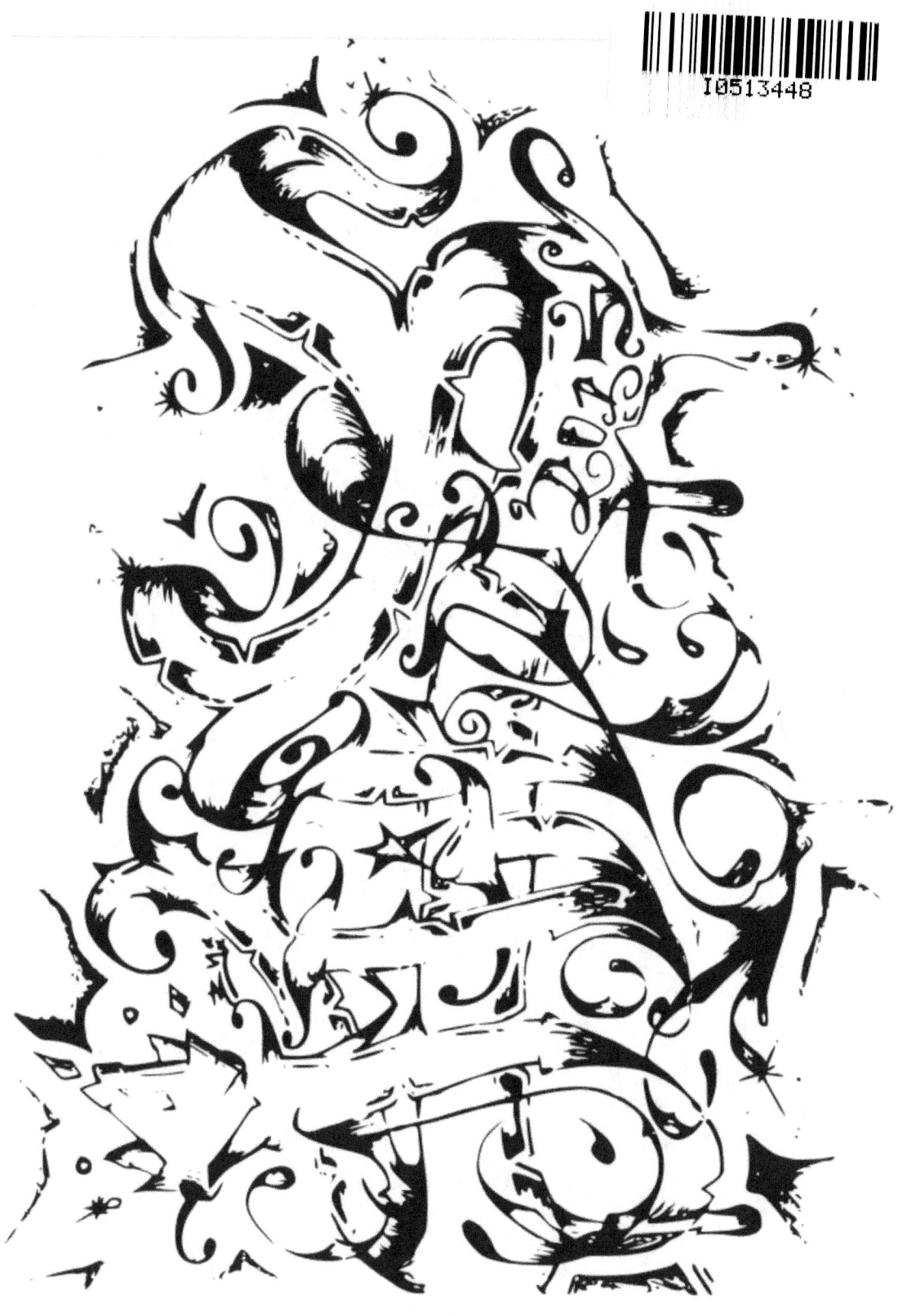

EXTREME COLORS:

An Adult "Grown up" Version of Coloring

Illustrated, Developed,
and Inspired By Michael Joyner

Version 1

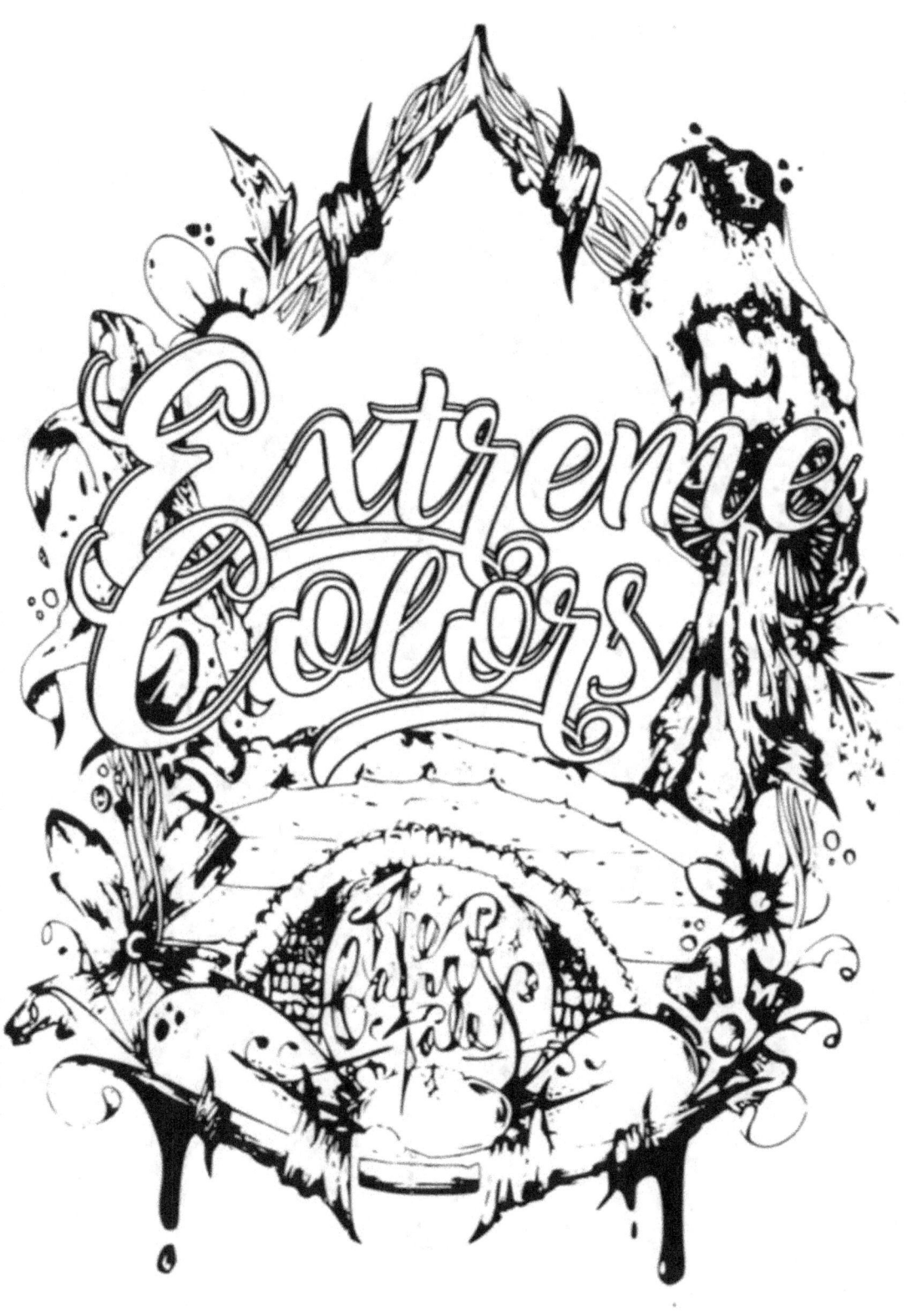

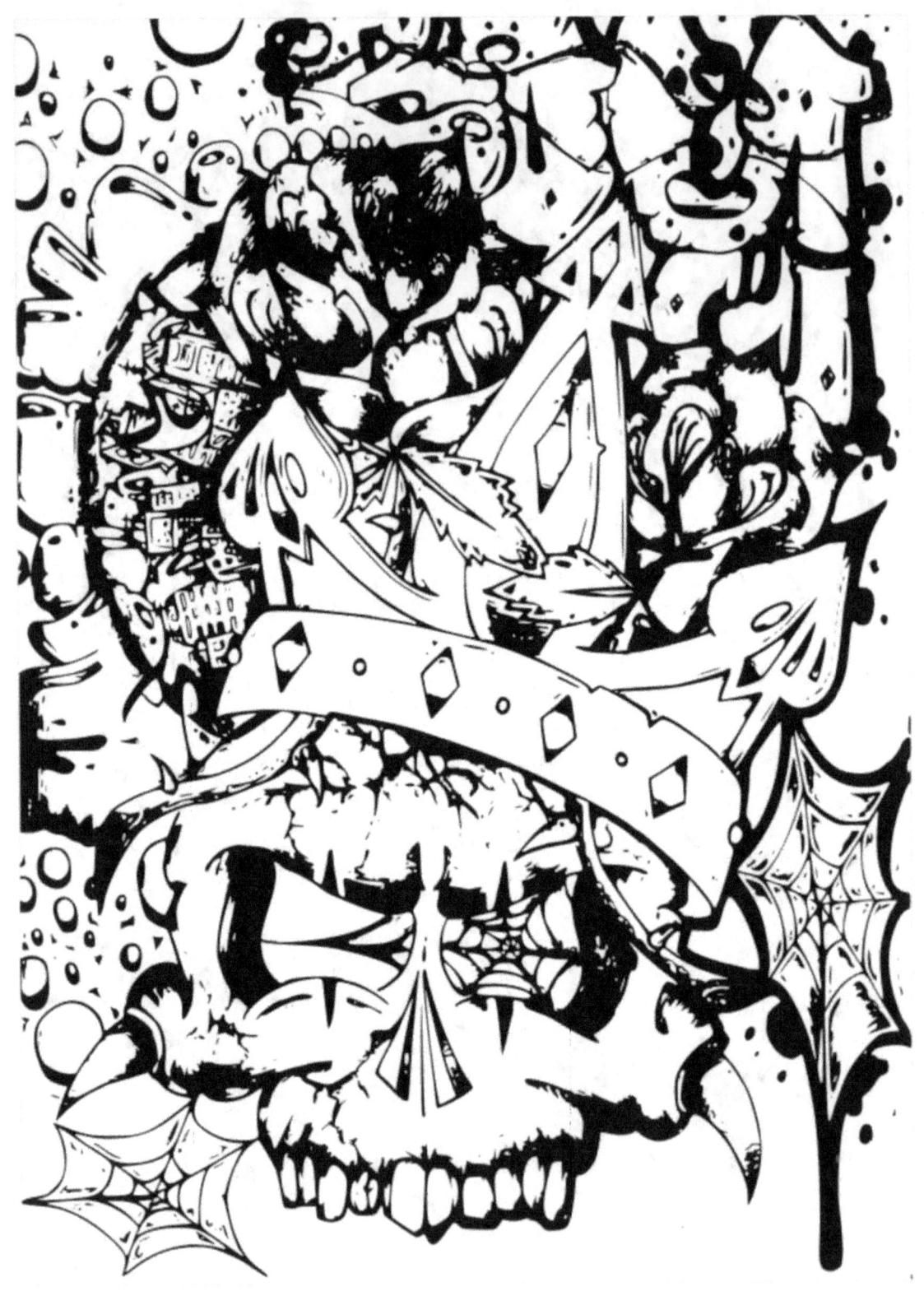

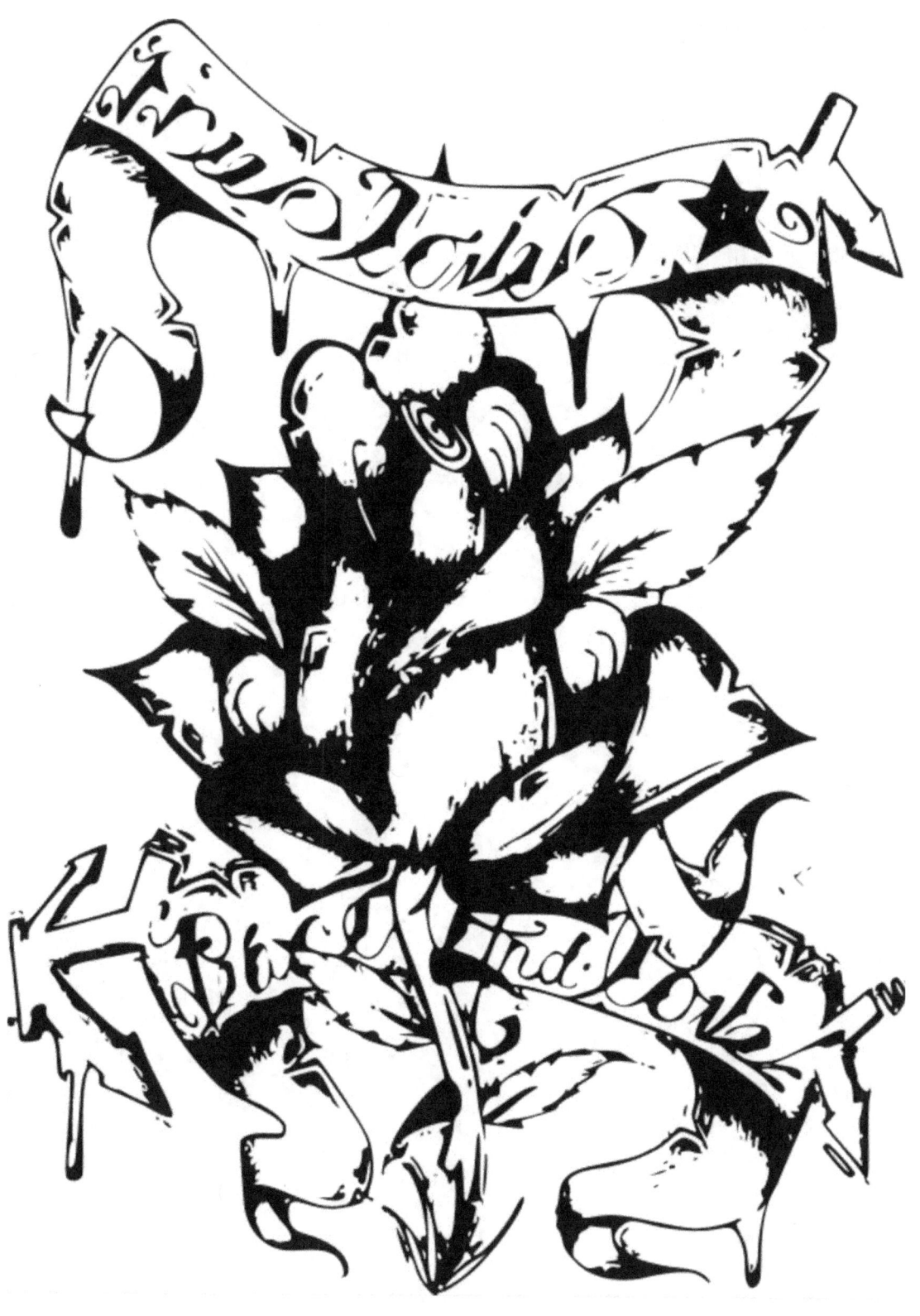

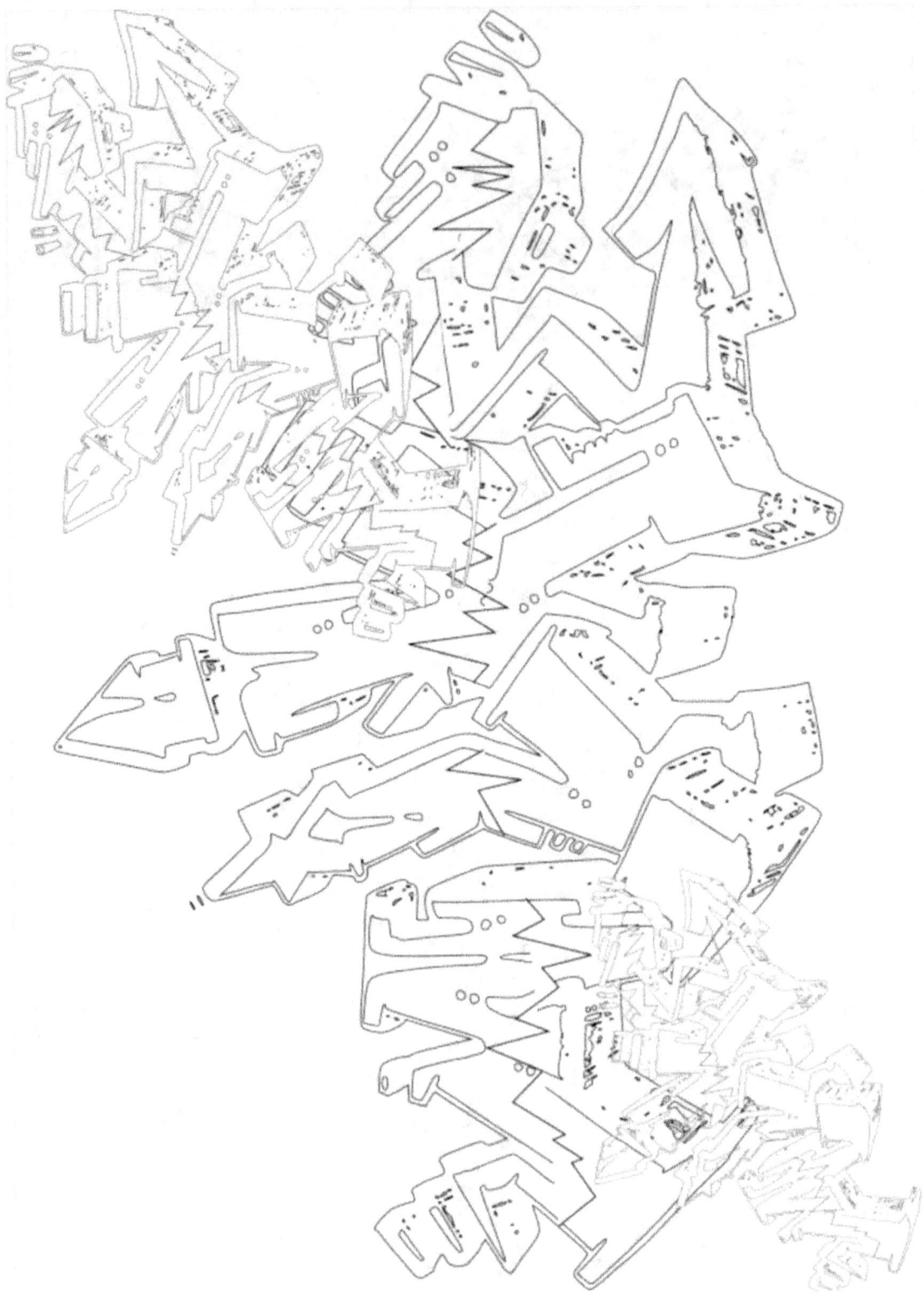

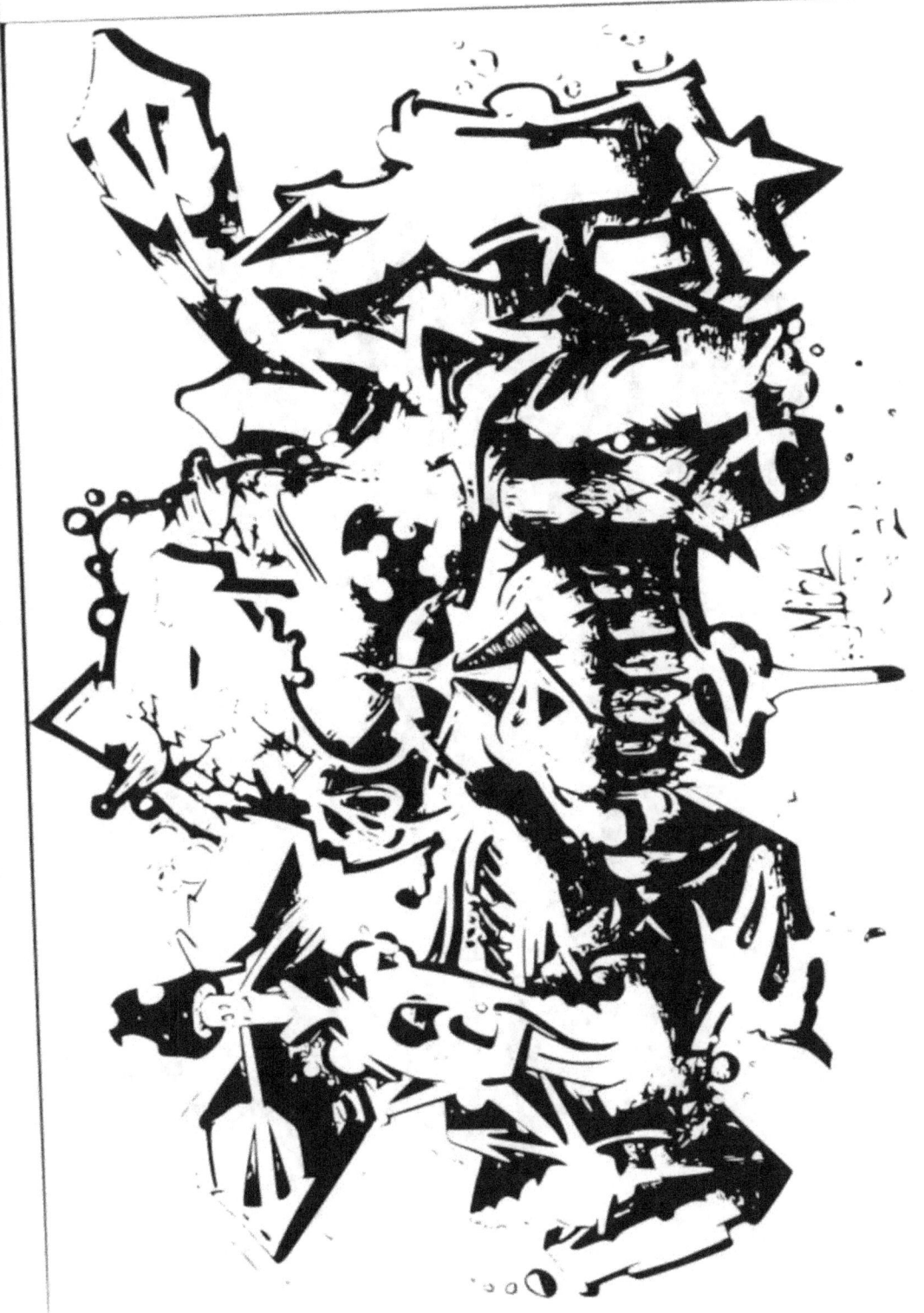

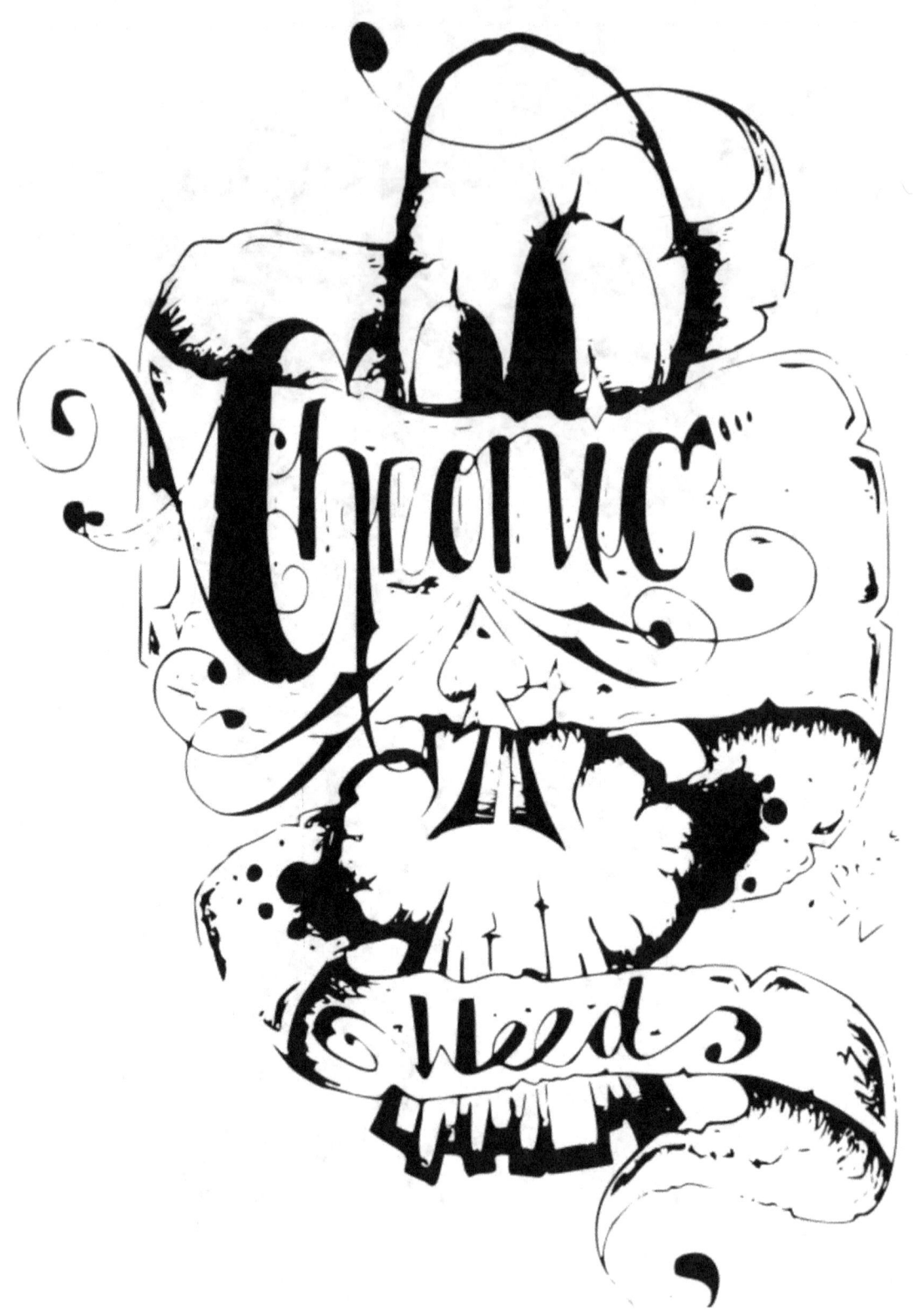

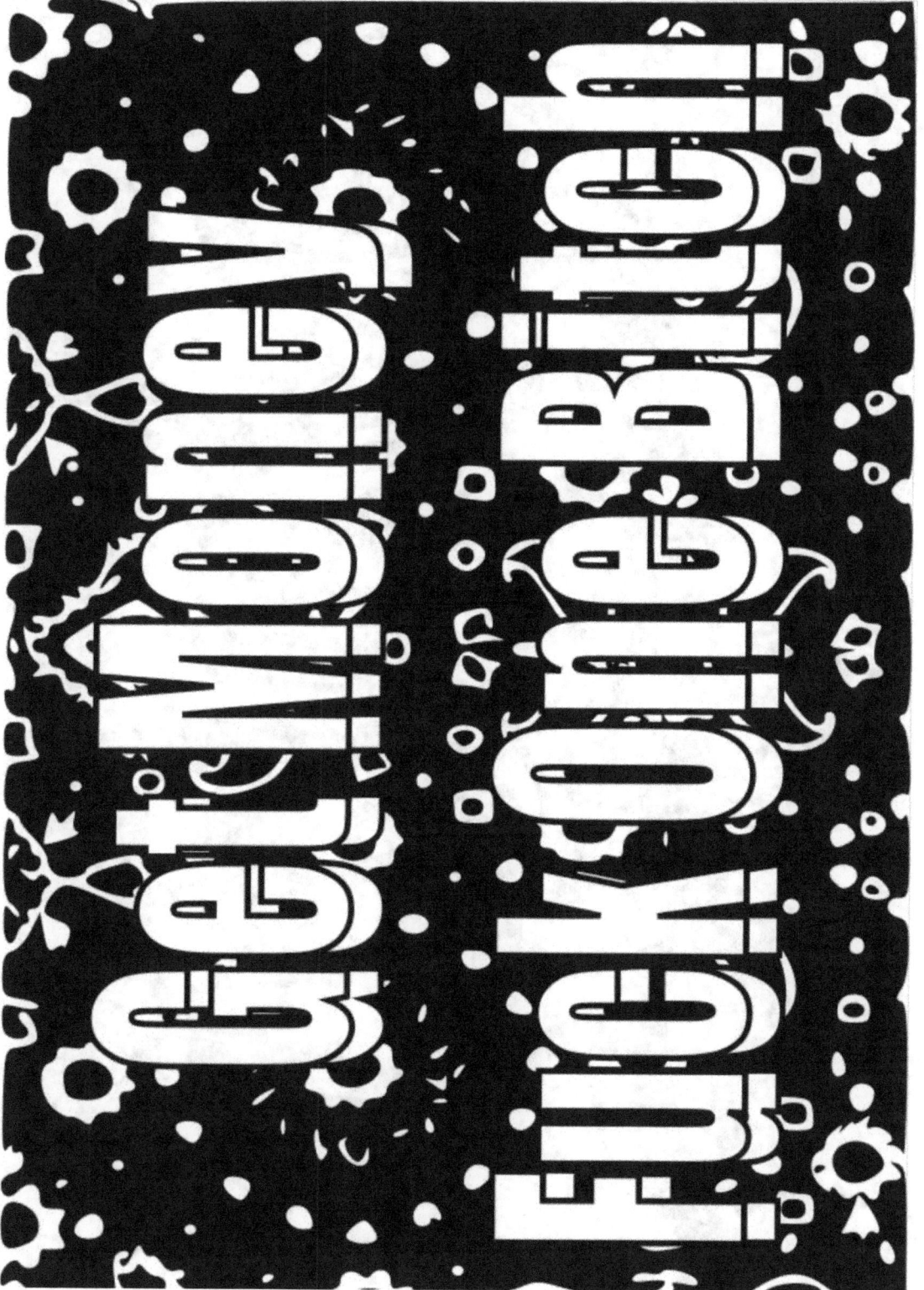

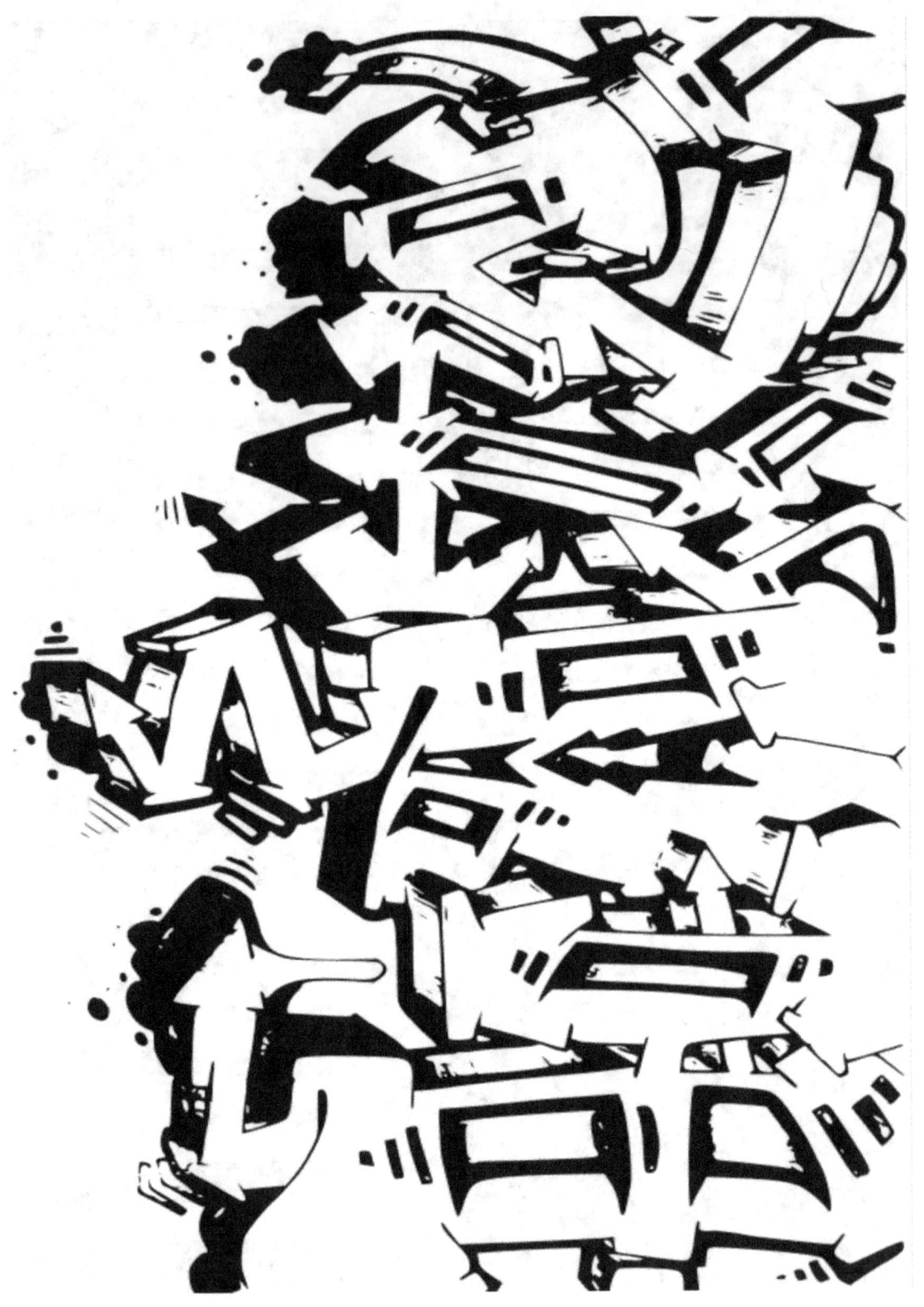

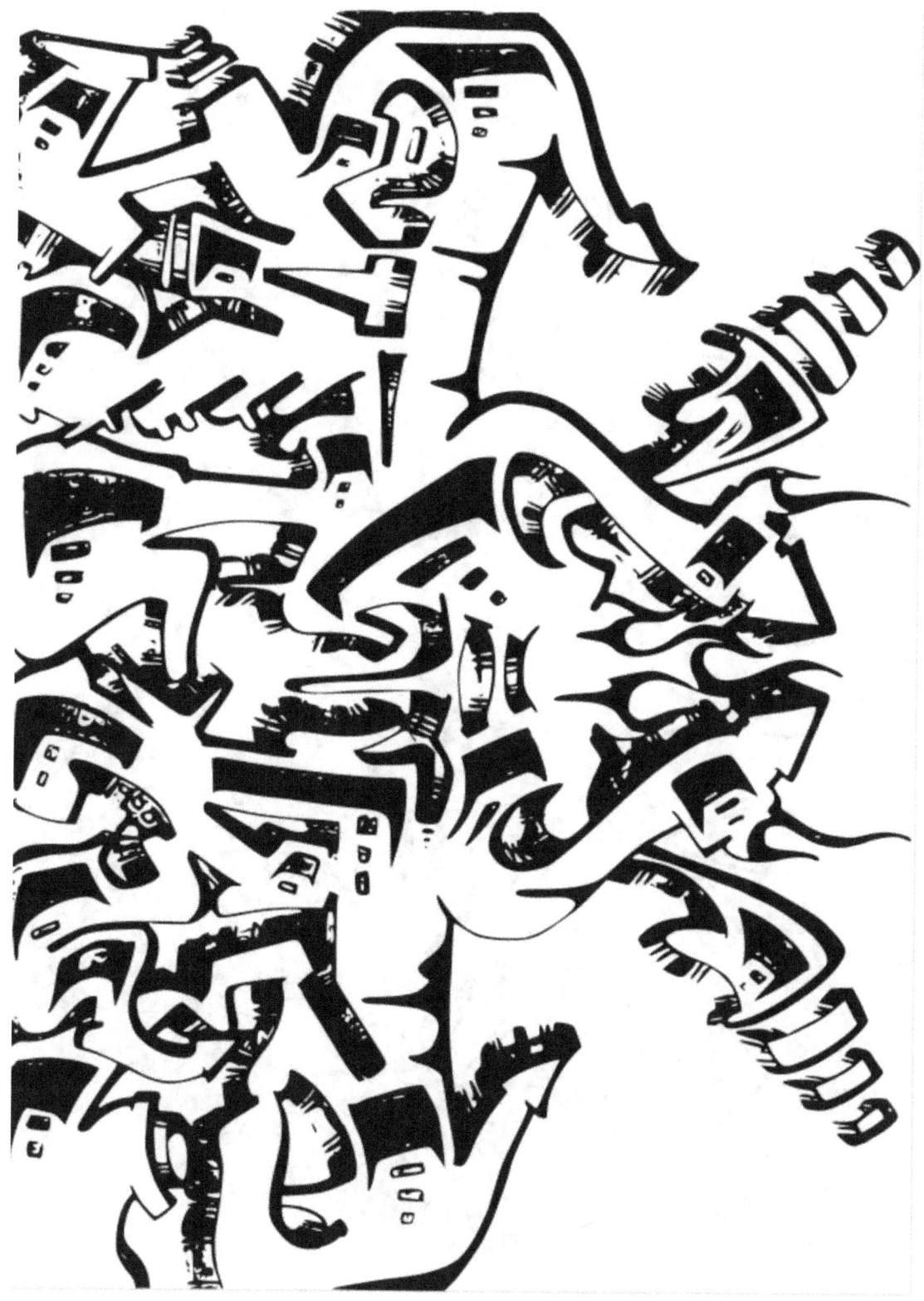

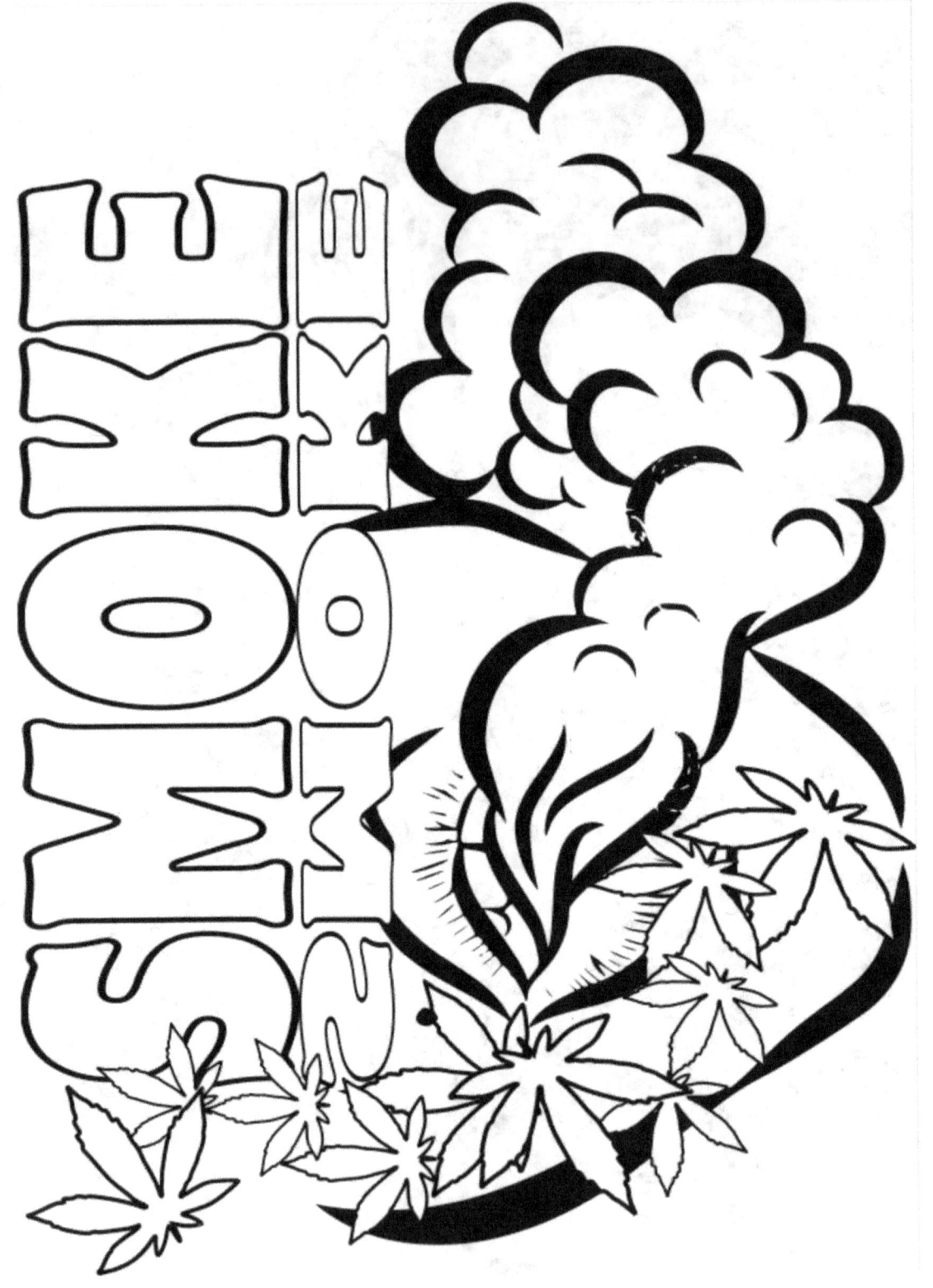

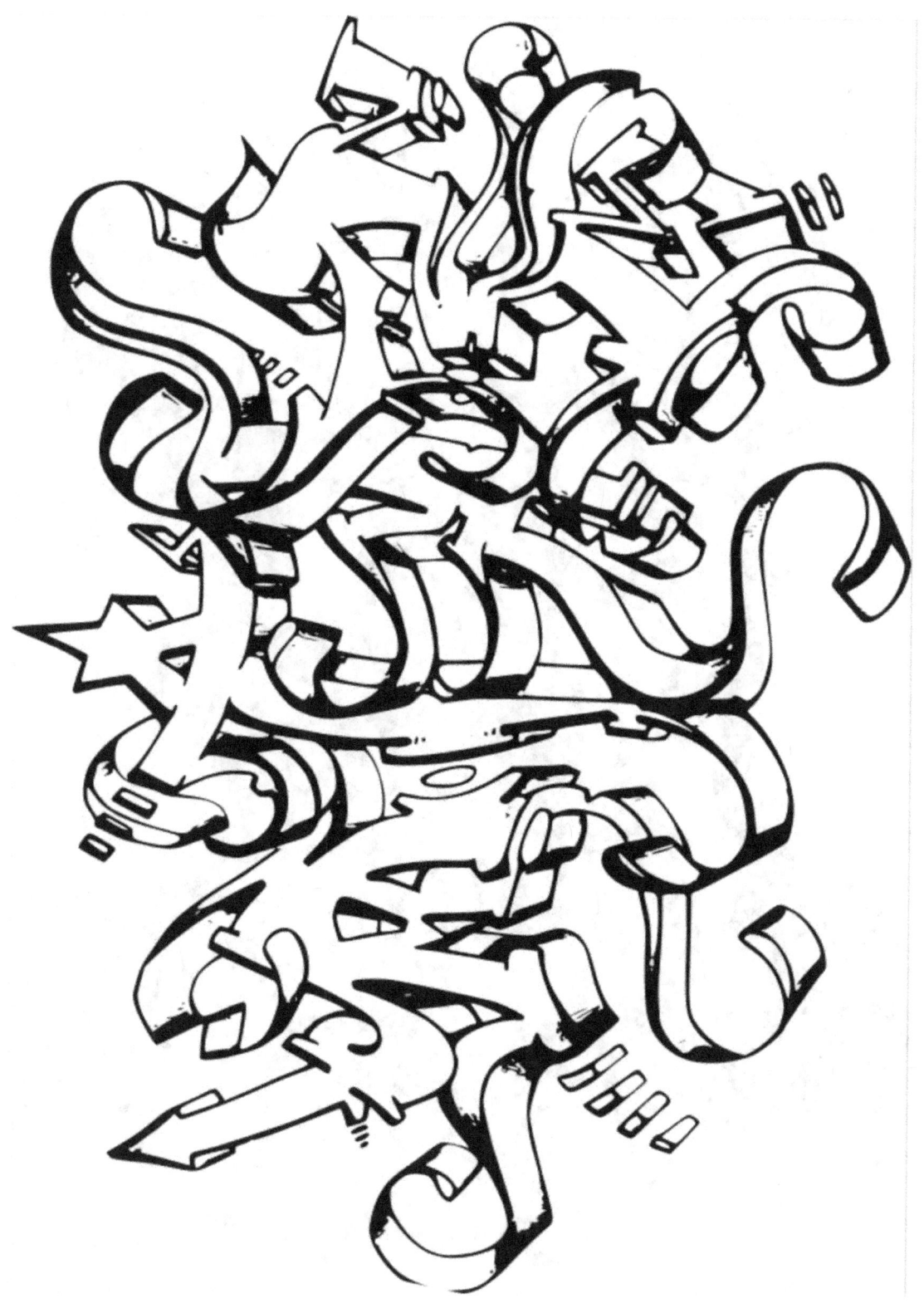

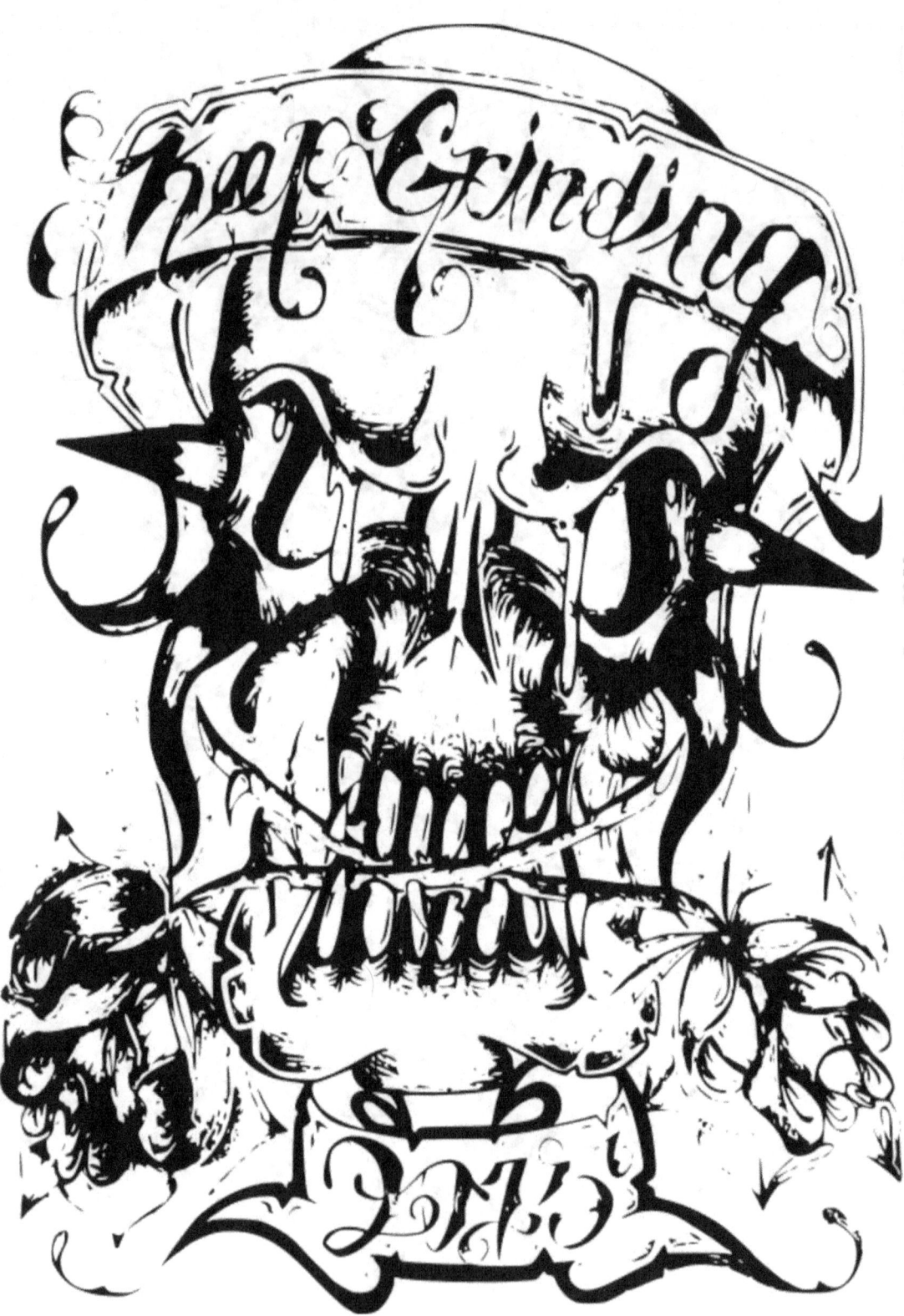

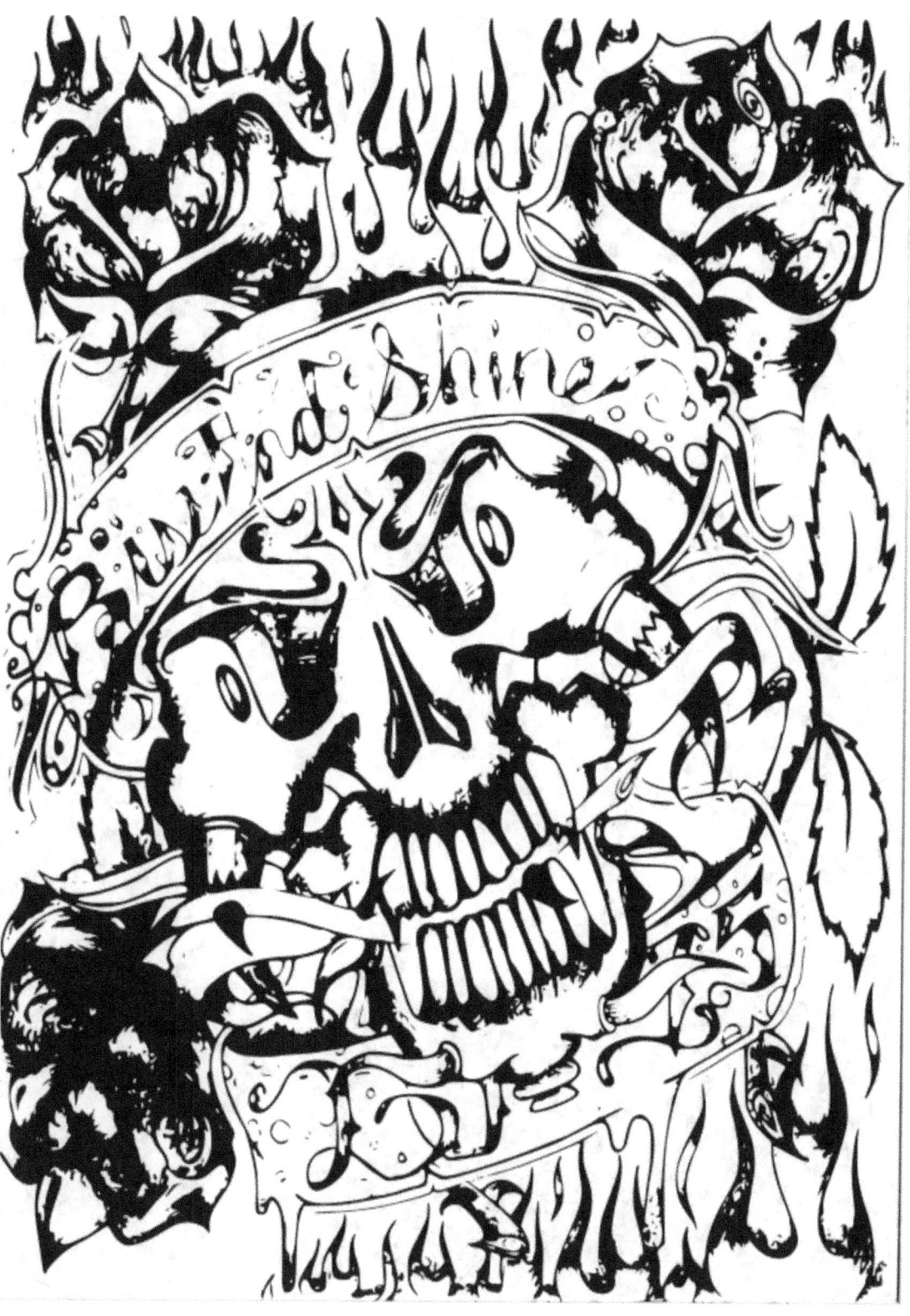

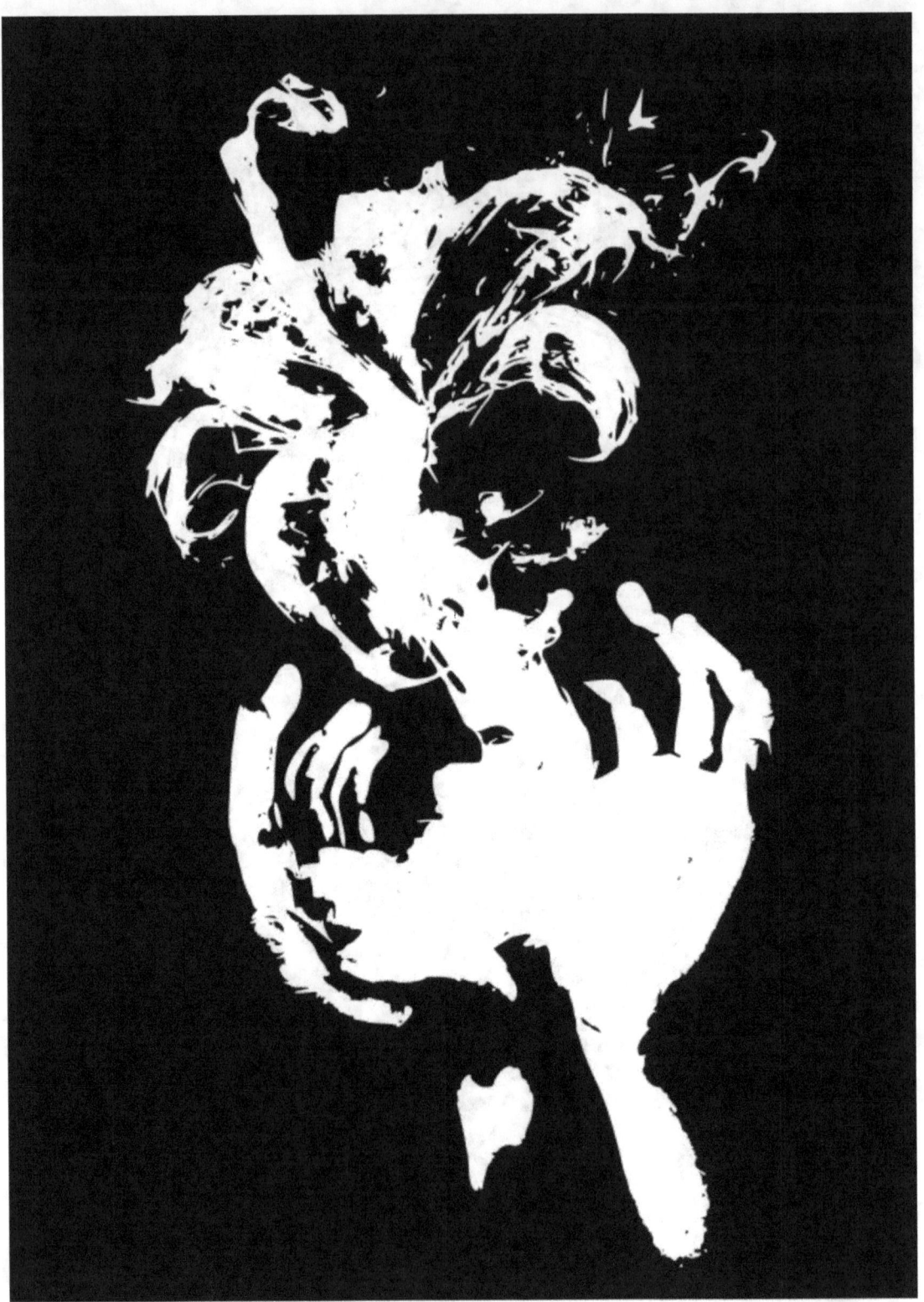

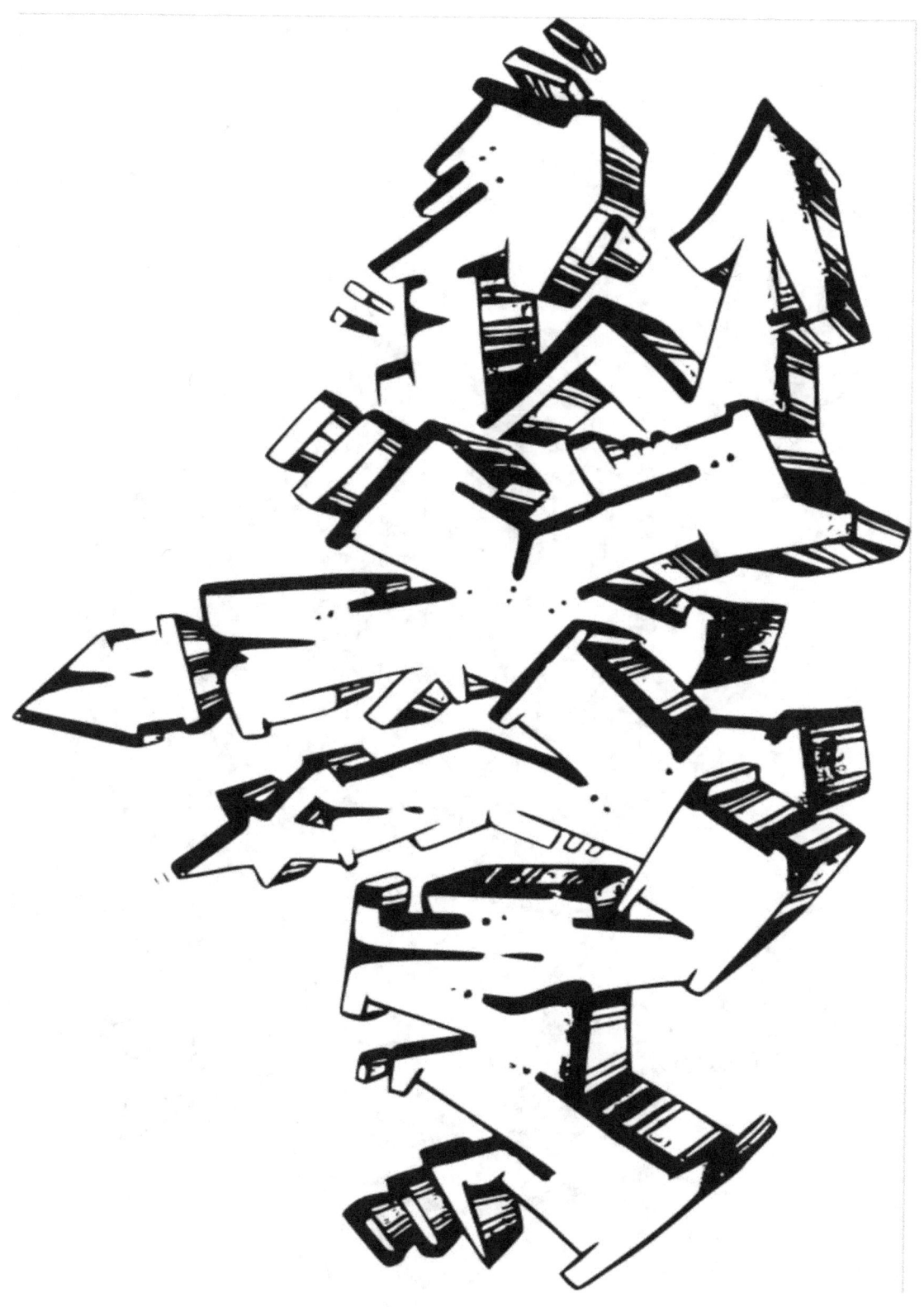

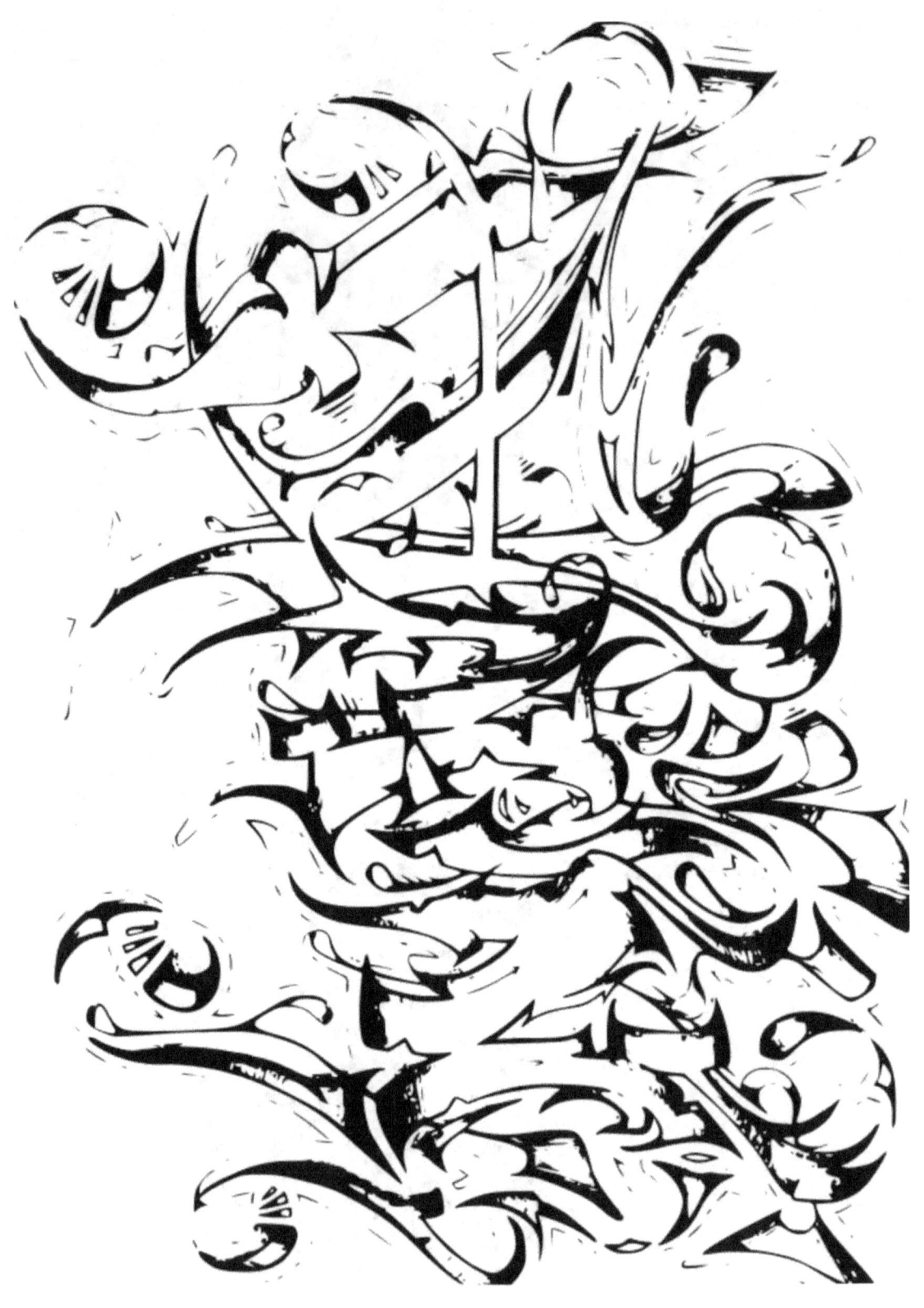

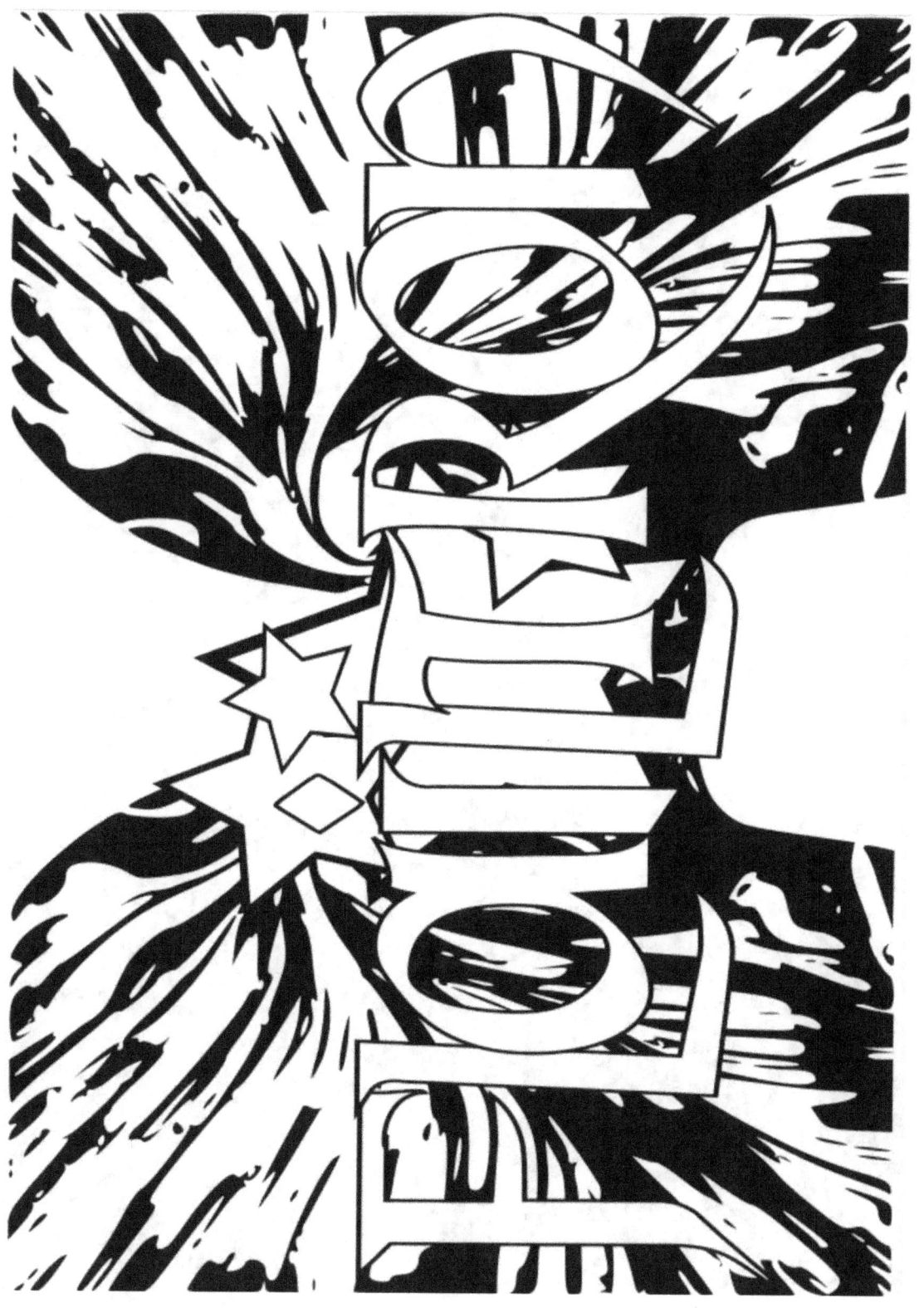

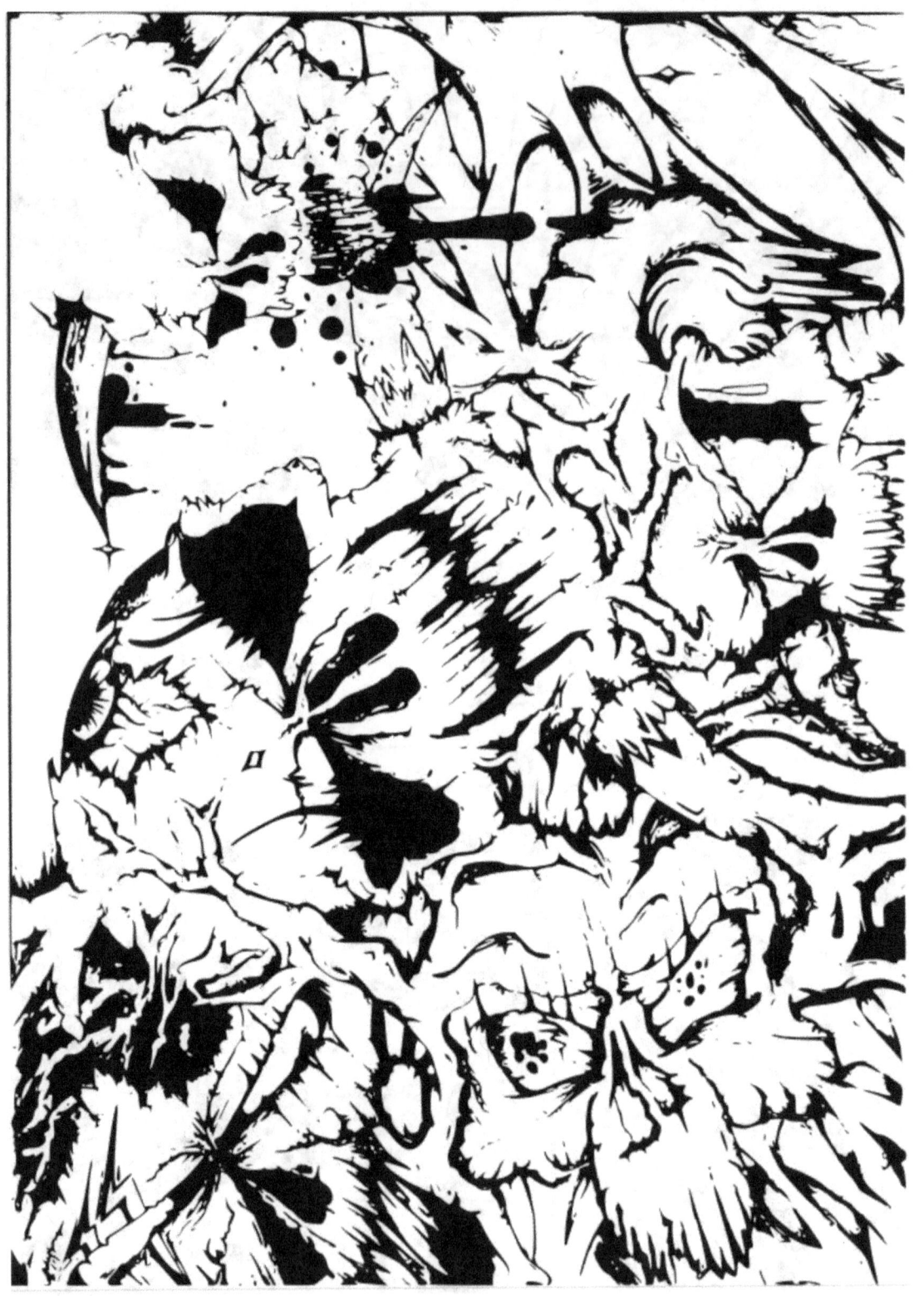

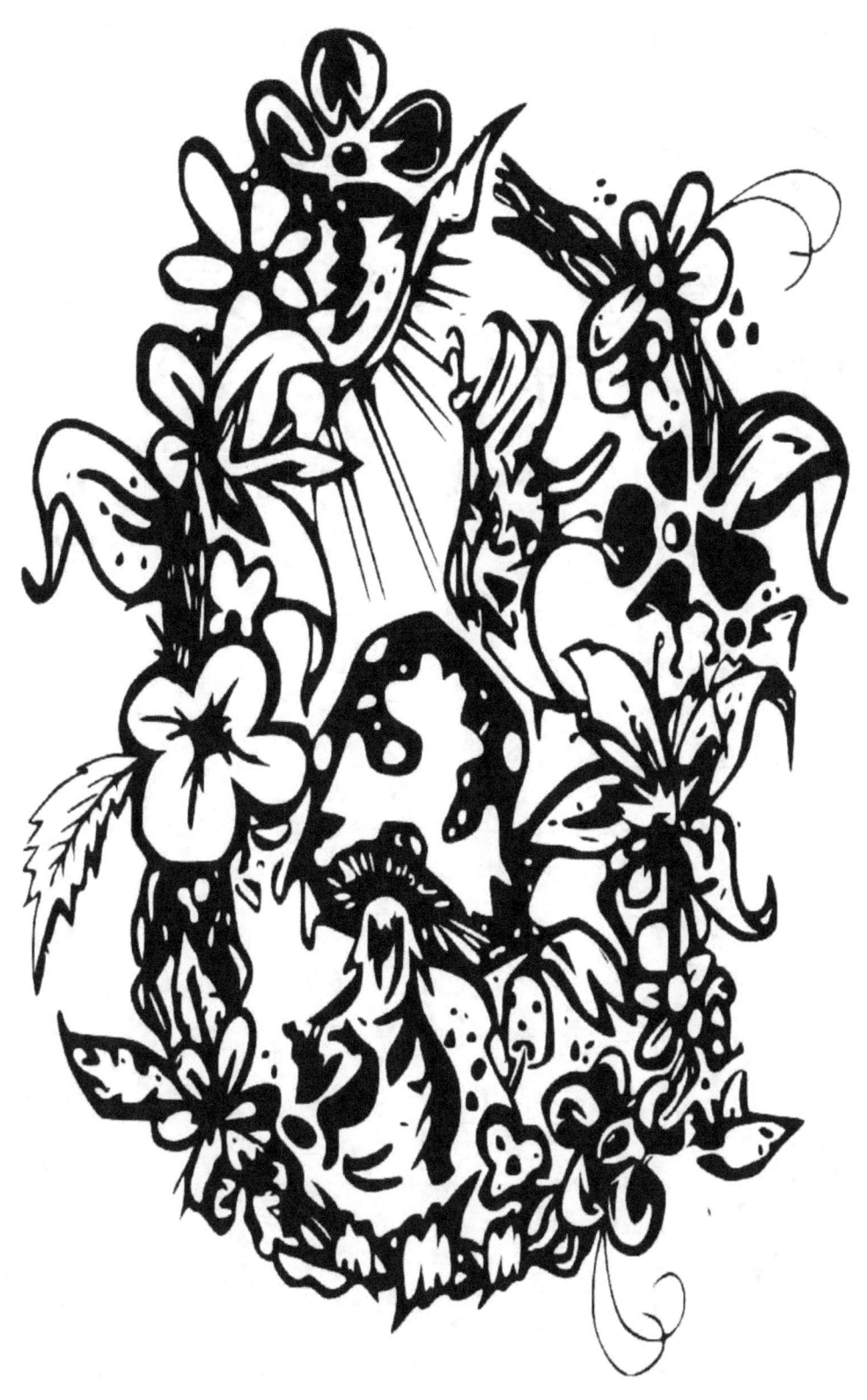

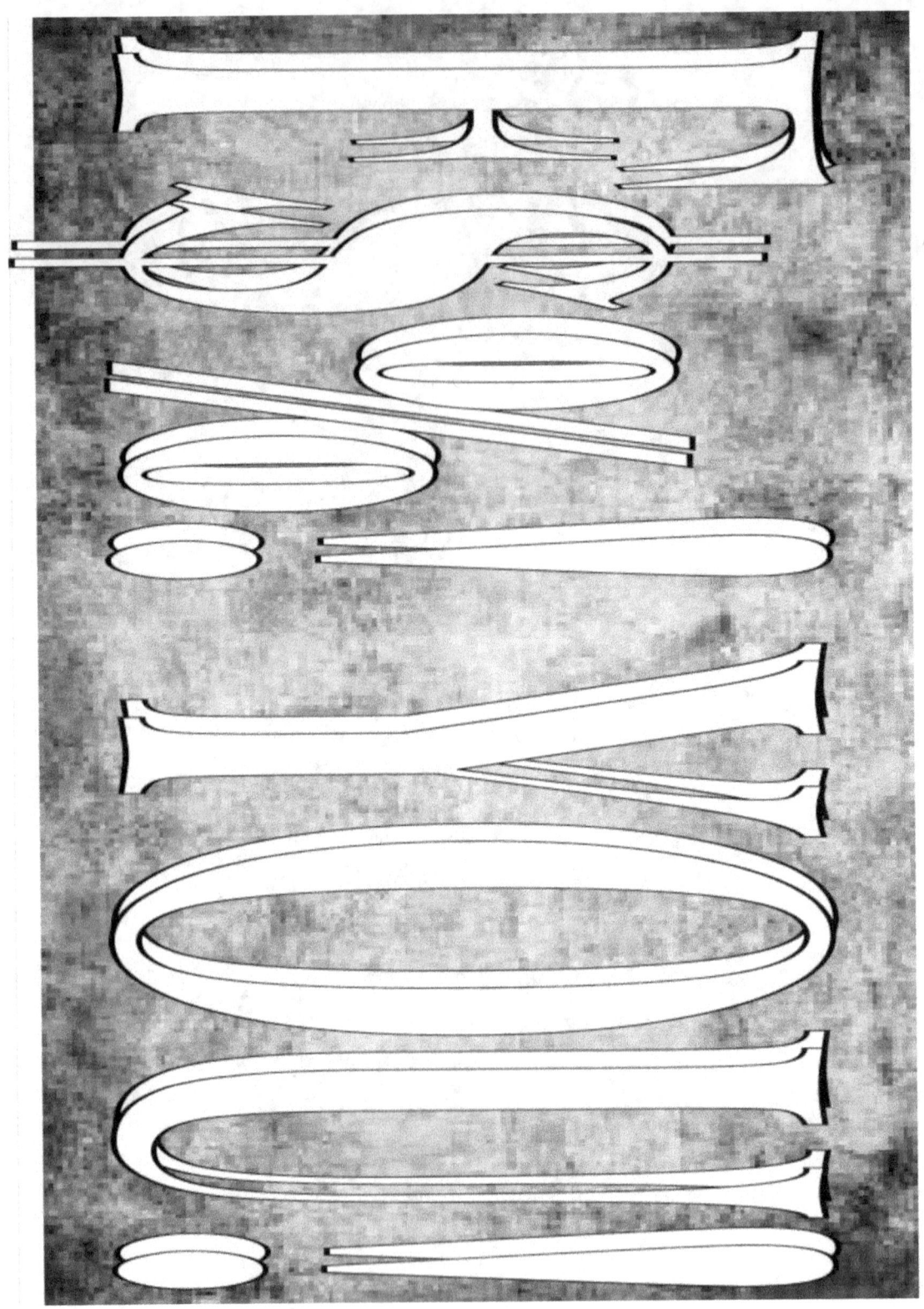

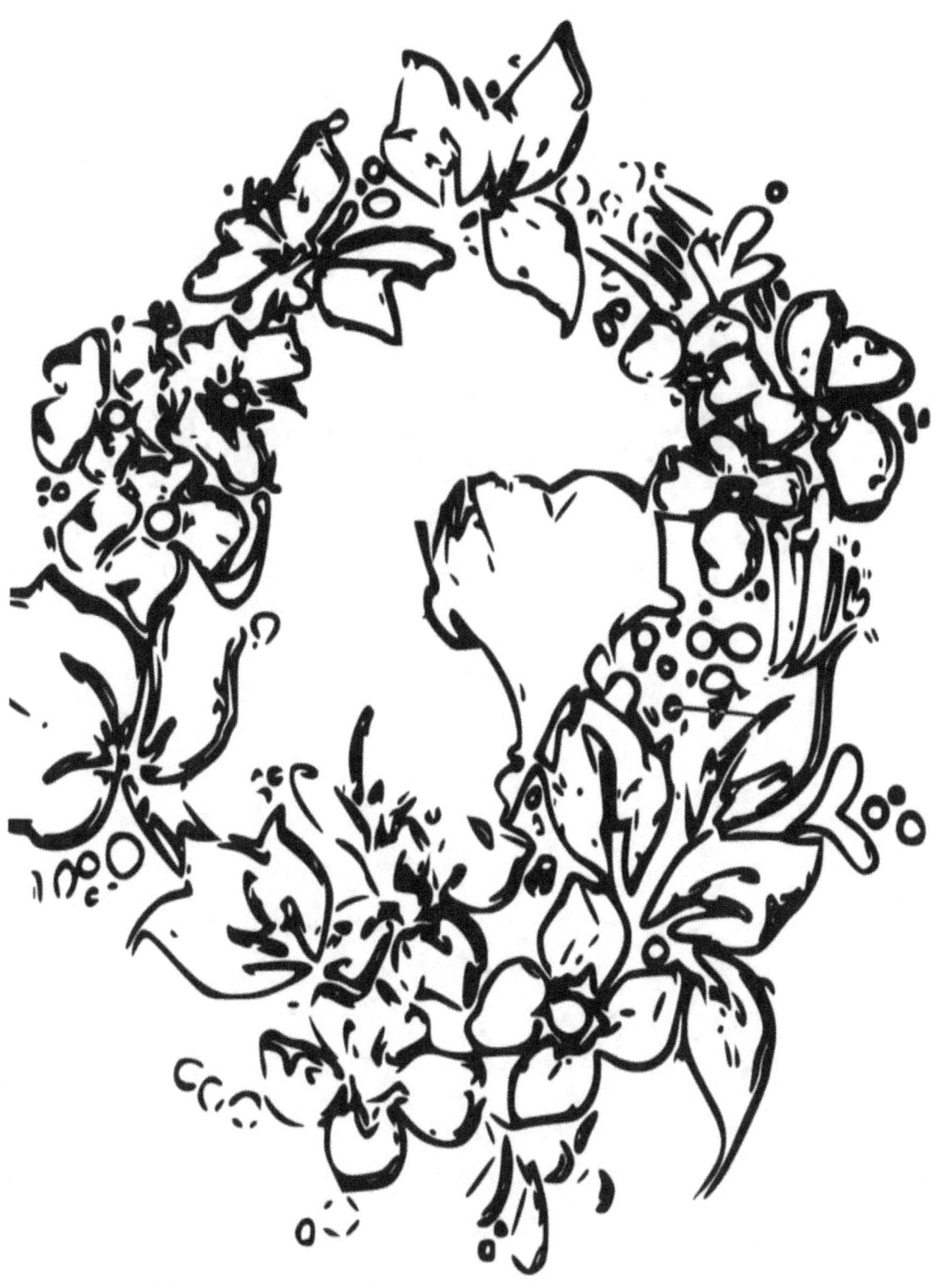

EXTREME COLORS:

An Adult "Grown up" Version of Coloring

Illustrated, Developed,
and Inspired By Michael Joyner

Version 1

www.ingramcontent.com/pod-product-compliance
Lightning Source LLC
Chambersburg PA
CBHW081022240526
45471CB00018B/3944